The
Emotionally
Healthy
Church

WORKBOOK

UPDATED *and* EXPANDED EDITION

The Emotionally Healthy Church

WORKBOOK

UPDATED *and* EXPANDED EDITION

8 STUDIES *for*
GROUPS OR INDIVIDUALS

Peter Scazzero

ZONDERVAN®

ZONDERVAN.com/
AUTHORTRACKER
follow your favorite authors

Emotionally Healthy Church Workbook
Updated and Expanded Edition
Copyright © 2010 by Peter L. Scazzero

Requests for information should be addressed to:

Zondervan, Grand Rapids, Michigan 49530

ISBN 978-0-310-32785-1

Interior design: Mark Sheeres

Printed in the United States of America

HB 08.23.2017

CONTENTS

Acknowledgments

I would like to give a special word of thanks to Dan Shin for his insightful and significant contribution to this study guide. Also, thanks to Chris Giammona, who gave a good portion of sweat equity to this project.

Finally, thanks to the New Life Fellowship Family, the soil out of which God has met us all in such a wonderful way.

Introduction and Overview

WELCOME

Welcome to a journey with Jesus Christ that will, I trust, change your life! The goal of this study guide is to enable you to apply the biblical truths and principles found in *The Emotionally Healthy Church: Updated and Expanded Edition* (Zondervan, 2010) to your personal life, small group, and church life. I wrote the book with leaders in mind, knowing that "as goes the leaders, so goes the church." Nonetheless, countless small groups and Sunday school classes have benefitted immensely from engaging the powerful, often neglected, biblical principles explored in this workbook.

The revolutionary assertion of this workbook is simple:

Emotional health and spiritual maturity are inseparable. It is not possible to be spiritually mature while remaining emotionally immature.

When Jesus trained the Twelve, he intentionally created experiences for them to walk in the truth. He sent them out two by two to preach (Matt. 10). He gave them words to pray (Luke 11). He led them to places they normally would avoid. He forced them to apply the message of the kingdom of God and not simply assent to it intellectually.

In the same way, discipleship that embraces emotional health requires that we *do* it, and not simply read about it. Therefore, each study includes at least one experience for you and/or the group to do. It is designed to take you to a "new place" in your walk with Christ, provoking you to pray and seek him in a fresh way.

This particular study guide takes you into the practical application of the seven principles of what it means to have Jesus Christ transform the emotional aspect of who you are. Our goal is that you would become a more loving, authentic human being—toward God, others, and yourself—and that you slow down your life to lead with integrity (Principle 7).

We are very excited that you are taking this step in your discipleship journey. Paul prays that the church in Ephesus might "grasp the immensity of this glorious way of life he has for [Christians]" (Eph. 1:18 MSG). This has been the fruit of this journey for my wife, Geri, and me in our relationships with God, each other, our family, our friends, our church, and the larger world. It is our prayer that as you take these next steps, God may lead you to more of his truth, because that alone sets us free!

HOW TO USE THIS STUDY GUIDE

- Ask participants to come with the recommended reading and/or assignment completed.

- Encourage small group members to use these studies as part of their devotional times during the week, praying and meditating on the texts and truths before the meeting. Ask them to note some rough answers to the questions before they come to the meeting. Working through the material in this workbook is their next important step in maturing spiritually.

- Give people the opportunity to share what is going on inside of them as an important step toward emotional health. Seek to create a climate of support and acceptance. For this reason, if your group is large, it's better to place people into smaller groups of 3–5, when appropriate, so that everyone has time to share.

- Notice that each study is divided into five sections:
  - Growing Connected
  - Starters
  - Bible Study
  - Applications/Exercises
  - Going Deeper
- Seek the Spirit's guidance in pacing the discussion. (More specific suggestions for the small group leader/facilitator can be found on pages 11 – 12 of this guide.)

Overview

The seven principles are interrelated and build upon each other. Before we go into each principle, I want to provide you with an overview of how they fit together to form the entire premise that emotional health cannot be separated from spiritual maturity.

Principle 1: Look beneath the Surface
I become aware that the ways I respond, relate, and react in my daily life often involve a lot more than my first-glance thoughts and intentions of the moment.

Principle 2: Break the Power of the Past
I realize the degree to which my family of origin has shaped how I see the world, handle conflict, and deal with emotions.

Principle 3: Live in Brokenness and Vulnerability
I realize that we are all broken people and that none of us comes to Jesus Christ with a "Get-Out-of-Discipleship-for-Free" card. We all need to be profoundly retrained, retaught, reworked, and reshaped under his lordship and grace.

Principle 4: Receive the Gift of Limits
In my brokenness, I begin to see that God has blessed me with limitations that I must learn to embrace and receive instead of fight and deny. I was born with certain limits, others were thrust upon me, and still others were a result of my own choices.

Principle 5: Embrace Grieving and Loss
In seeing the limits of my life, especially the ones over which I had no control, I enlarge my soul by grieving the reality that I can never do and be all that I've hoped for on this side of heaven.

Principle 6: Make Incarnation Your Model for Loving Well
Now being better acquainted with myself, my own limits, my own past, and my own brokenness, I can hold onto myself, and love others more freely by entering into their world without losing my true self.

Principle 7: Slow Down to Lead with Integrity
We must slow down our hurried lives in order to have integrity in four key areas: our relationship with God, with ourselves, with our spouses (when applicable), and in our leadership of others.

Guidelines for Small Group Leaders/Facilitators

1. Work through the material and exercises for each study before you arrive. You are on a journey with the rest of the group, allowing God into the deep parts of your life like the rest of the group. Relax. You don't need to be an expert.

2. Participate in the group as a member, sharing what God has taught you through your own individual study.

3. Spend time focusing on the passage being studied. Read the corresponding chapter in the book *The Emotionally Healthy Church*: *Updated and Expanded Edition* (2010).

4. Read aloud the introductory section at the beginning of each study. This will orient the group to the session topic.

5. Seek to be sensitive to members of the group who may be concerned that you are "compromising Scripture" or "elevating emotions." This can be threatening to some people who have never given themselves permission to feel or express themselves. Ask God for grace to create a safe, loving, accepting atmosphere.

6. Be careful not to dominate the discussion. Encourage each participant to share.

7. Freely say "I don't know" when someone asks you a question you can't answer. You too are on the journey of integrating emotional health and biblical spirituality.

8. Pray. God changes lives by the Holy Spirit in response to believing prayer. Expect the Holy Spirit to change each person's life. He is the one responsible for the growth of each member of your group. Be sure to pray at the beginning and end of each gathering.

9. Respect confidentiality. Ask the group members in the first meeting to hold in confidence what people share in the group. "Let what you hear here, stay here."

Discipleship's Missing Link

Reading: Introduction and Chapter 1

 ## GROWING CONNECTED

Taking an "Emotional Snapshot"

1. Divide an 8½" x 11" piece of paper into four boxes, and write the following words at the top of each box.

Glad	Sad
Mad	Anxious/Afraid

In each box, draw a picture or write down in words the thing(s) you are Glad, Mad, Sad, or Anxious/Afraid about in your life right now. Give yourself five minutes.

2. In groups of four or as a whole group, have people share their pictures and/or words with each other. (Have each person pick one category to share if time is limited.)

 **STARTERS**

The summary of *The Emotionally Healthy Church* is this:

> **Emotional health and spiritual maturity are inseparable.
> It is not possible to be spiritually mature while
> remaining emotionally immature.**

3. How does being aware of your "Emotional Snapshot" relate to your discipleship in Christ?

 **BIBLE STUDY**

4. Read Psalm 69:1–12, 19–21, and 29–31. Seek to step into David's shoes. What emotions was he feeling as he wrote this psalm? Circle any that you find in the list below, or add your own beneath the box.

Joy	Depression
Love	Grief
Gladness	Hopelessness
Thanksgiving	Despair
Certainty	Pain
Peace	Helplessness
Trust	Confusion
Playfulness	Rejection
Accepted	Anger
	Bitterness

David: Unafraid to Bare His Soul

The Bible presents David as a man after God's own heart, yet a quick reading of the Psalms shows us that his emotional world was very human and very broken. David bares his soul in these heart-wrenching poems, and by placing them in his Scriptures, God seems to be saying: "To have true intimacy with me is not to paint a 'Praise the Lord' smile on your face 24/7, but to be so trusting in my love and embrace that you are free and safe to share all your feelings with me—no matter how messy or confusing they might seem to you."

5. If David visited your church or small group and presented Psalm 69 as his testimony, would you take it as a sign of spiritual weakness or spiritual strength, immaturity or maturity? Explain.

6. How would you react if David opened up in this way in your small group? How would you feel if David were your pastor, sharing this with your congregation at a Sunday worship service?

7. What about your life experiences, family history, or bad religious teachings may have caused you to deny or repress your feelings rather than bring them to God as David did?

Jesus: A Savior with Emotions

When you look at the Scriptures with this new paradigm in hand, you will see that Jesus was anything but an "emotionally frozen Messiah." He expressed emotion with unashamed, unembarrassed freedom.

Consider the broad range of emotions Jesus experienced.

- He shed tears. (Luke 19:41)
- He was filled with joy. (Luke 10:21)
- He grieved and felt sorrow. (Mark 14:34; Luke 7:13)
- He was angry. (Mark 3:5)
- He showed astonishment and wonder. (Mark 6:6; Luke 7:9)
- He felt distress. (Mark 3:5; Luke 12:50)

APPLICATIONS/EXERCISES

The diagram below illustrates the different aspects of what it means to be made in God's image. Conformity to Christ includes all these areas.

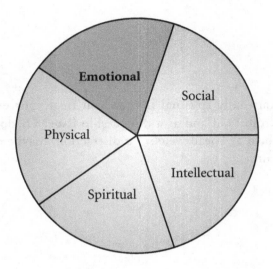

"In the minds of many today, the repression of feelings and emotions has been elevated to the status of Spirit or virtue. Denying anger, ignoring pain, skipping over depression, running from loneliness, avoiding confusing doubts, and turning off our sexuality have become a way of spiritual life." (*EHC*, p. 57)

APPLICATIONS/EXERCISES

8. What would your life be like if a slice of the pie on the previous page were missing? How would it prevent you from living a truly Christlike life?

9. In your daily spiritual life, do you treat your emotions as a gift from God and as a discipleship issue? Or do you tend to see them as "dead weight," a distraction, maybe even a curse? Explain.

10. Complete the following sentence stem: I am beginning to realize ...

WRAPPING UP

We saw how people in the Bible, such as David and even Jesus himself, enjoyed full and vibrant emotional lives. Out of their security in

God's love and grace, they were able to freely express their feelings to themselves, to others, and to their heavenly Father.

Embracing our emotions can be a difficult and confusing thing to do. Short-term spiritual "victories" seem to come easier, cleaner, and prettier when we bury and stuff our feelings. Learning how to hear what God is doing and saying to us through our emotions can appear to be a waste of time.

Join the apostle Paul in praying that Christ be formed in every part of you — including your emotional life (Gal. 4:19) — so that you can fully reflect the image of God.

 ## GOING DEEPER

- Complete the "Inventory of Emotional/Spiritual Maturity" in the appendix at the end of this workbook (p.75). Remember, it's completely normal and expected to score higher in certain principles than others. God often grows us in seasons, dealing with one issue at a time in our lives. The better response to these "gaps" is acknowledging that they exist and exploring what we can do to grow through them.

- This week, go back to the list of emotions that Jesus experienced and focus on a few that don't fit so well with your ideas of what Jesus is like. Consider how you handle those emotions when they come up in your life. Allow God to let the reality of Jesus' vibrant emotional life sink in. Ask God to grant you the grace to embrace the fullness of your humanity and to share in the freedom of Jesus to experience your emotions and feelings.

FOR NEXT TIME

- Read chapter 5.
- Do the "Inventory of Emotional/Spiritual Maturity."

Principle 1: *Look Beneath the Surface*
Reading: Chapter 5

In Study 1, we began to see how today's approach to Christian discipleship can sometimes result in a rather lopsided life. Many of us are strong in certain aspects of faith, but weak in the emotional components of biblical spirituality.

In this study, we will begin our journey through the Seven Principles. It starts when I "look beneath the surface" and realize how my "iceberg" shapes the ways I respond, relate, and react to people and situations in my daily life.

🌿 GROWING CONNECTED

Only about 10 percent of an iceberg is visible above the surface. That is the part of our lives of which we are aware. It is also what we do that people can see — go to church, attend a small group, be courteous to one another, give financially, and so on. Deep beneath the surface of our lives, however, are layers of childhood wounds, unconscious motivations and fears, defenses, and memories/experiences we have forgotten.

1. What is one of your great fears as you consider taking a serious look at the "iceberg" in your life?

 **STARTERS**

Facing the Truth Can Be Hard

As human beings, God created us as complex and intricate creatures. We have many different aspects to who we are (emotional, spiritual, etc.), but we also have many different layers. In our daily decisions, all sorts of motivations, thoughts, and impulses are at work. Some we are conscious of, but others we are not. Ever since the fall, we human beings have been running away from the full truth about ourselves.

---

2. Although we know that the truth sets us free (John 8:32), why do you think unmasked honesty is so difficult for people? In what ways or situations is it difficult for you?

3. Why do we need a personal experience of God's unconditional love for us in order to search the "deep insides" of our lives and come out of hiding?

 **BIBLE STUDY**

Jesus knew that each of us is a walking iceberg, and he had a knack for taking people below the surface into the depths of their lives. Read John 4:7–18.

4. How does Jesus move the Samaritan woman from surface concerns to the deeper issues of her life and faith?

5. To what relational pattern was Jesus pointing the woman's attention? What were the symptoms in her life?

6. How would you describe her response to Jesus' exposing her iceberg?

How do you tend to respond when people or circumstances expose hidden layers underneath the visible surface of your iceberg? Explain.

Applications/Exercises

Finding the Patterns

Patterns in our lives and relationships are often a sign that we're acting out from deep places in our iceberg. They usually reveal a "bug" in our emotional programming, something that plays out over and over again in our lives. If you or a close loved one notice a "pattern of unhealth" emerging in your life, that is usually a good sign that something's amiss in your internal wiring.

---

7. Try your best to complete the statements below and at the top of the next page.

   "Most of the time, I feel as if I am _____."
   (e.g., invisible, unimportant, failing, guilty)

   "What often happens to me in relationships is _____."
   (e.g., people leave me, take advantage of me, betray me)

   "Why do others at work or school keep on _____ me?"
   (e.g., ignoring, expecting unrealistic things of, criticizing)

"When I am under stress, I often find myself _____."
(e.g., fighting, angry, medicating myself, blaming others, losing myself in an unhealthy way)

"When I think about the future, I feel _____."
(e.g., depressed, anxious, lost, unsure)

Asking the "Whys"

It takes the grace of God to get at the bottom of our iceberg. Thankfully, there are "disciplines of reflection" to help us in walking in that grace. One of these is the "Why?" or "What's going on?" question. As we notice patterns in our feelings, situations, and relationships that emerge in our lives, God desires that we ask ourselves the "Why?" question in the safety of his presence.

---

8. Share a recent situation in which you have felt some anger, frustration, fear, shame, bitterness, hate, grief, or jealousy. Use the questions below as a starting point to get at "What's going on?"

   - Rage/Anger: "How was I hurt?"
   - Frustration: "What did I feel helpless about?"
   - Shame: "What was I hiding?"
   - Resentment: "What did I expect or hope for?"
   - Depression: "What did I lose?"
   - Jealousy: "Where did I feel inadequate?"

9. What is one step you can take this week to look beneath the iceberg in your life? Be specific.

Wrapping Up

It takes courage to ask yourself: What am I really feeling in this situation? What's really going on here? This is especially so when you are experiencing a "negative" emotion such as anger, shame, bitterness, hate, grief, jealousy, fear, or depression. Ask yourself once again: How might God be speaking or coming to me through these emotions?

Going Deeper

- Think about your life over the last few years. See if you can discern any patterns that emerge in your relationships, family life, ministry, or work. Write down each pattern and begin to ask God to open your eyes to the "whys" behind them. Keep a journal. Again, bring them to him in prayer.

For Next Time

- Read chapter 6.

Principle 2: *Break the Power of the Past*
Reading: Chapter 6

In Study 2, we learned that when it comes to our lives, there's a lot more than meets the eye. Like an iceberg, there are huge chunks of who we are that remain hidden beneath the surface.

In this study, we're going to see how the past is related to the present, and how the family in which we grew up has a lot to do with how we're put together at the bottom of our icebergs. The Bible teaches that both blessings and curses can be passed on in families from generation to generation.

GROWING CONNECTED

1. Do you remember being annoyed or hurt by something your parents or primary caregivers did, then vowing to yourself, "I will never be like this when I grow up"? Yet in our adult life we find ourselves struggling with the same character defects and unhealthy relational patterns as our parents did. Share one example.

STARTERS

Consider the genogram of Abraham below.

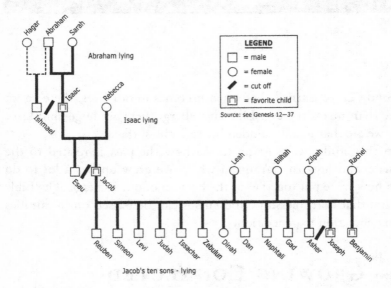

2. In each generation in Abraham's line, identify:

   a. the pattern of deception

   b. the favorite child or scapegoat

   c. sibling rivalry (tension between brothers)

3. How do you see sins and destructive patterns passed on in this family?

"Ten Commandments" of Our Family of Origin

4. Growing up, each one of our families operated under a set of "commandments." Some of them were spoken and spelled out; others were unspoken and "understood." Take ten minutes to jot down any rules, attitudes, and underlying assumptions your family had in two or three of the ten areas listed below — spoken or unspoken. Share one with the group, and tell how it continues to influence you today.

   Examples:

   - Money: "It's okay to spend it on others, but not on yourself."
   - Success: "It's getting into the best schools."
   - Expressing Anger: "When you are angry, it is a sin."
   - Loss and Grief: "You are not allowed to be sad or depressed."

"Ten Commandments" of My Family of Origin

1. Money: _____

2. Success: _____

3. God: _____

4. Gender Roles: _____

5. Marriage: _____

6. Complimenting/Praising: _____

7. Sex: _____

8. Play and Recreation: _____

9. Expressing Anger: _____

10. Loss and Grief: _____

BIBLE STUDY

Like everyone in the human race, our ultimate descent is from the family tree of Adam and Eve. Read Genesis 3:1–13.

5. Describe the sin of Adam and Eve (vv. 1–7). What are the consequences of that choice in their relationships with God and each other (vv. 8–13)?

In what ways do you, at times, observe the same dynamics played out in your life today?

The Church as "New First Family"

Our family of origin is the single most powerful and formative influence that has shaped the person we are today. Therefore it makes sense that Christian discipleship is ultimately about transplanting someone from their family of origin and rooting them into the new family of Christ. Just as there were established ways of handling anger, money, conflict, sex, feelings, and the like, in our family of origin, so there are new ways of thinking and acting about these things in the family of God. Discipleship is a process of unlearning and relearning, because through Christ, we've been birthed into a new family tree!

6. What are one or two things that you believe God wants you to "relearn" in his family?

7. The church is a place where people bring their entire family histories with them through the door. What sorts of challenges does this present to functioning as a church family after God's own heart?

 ## APPLICATIONS/EXERCISES

8. Refer back to the " 'Ten Commandments' of Our Family of Origin" section (question 4). Take a few minutes to rewrite one or two of the family of origin commandments based on your understanding of what God teaches in Scripture. Share one with the group.

Example:

- Success: "In God's family, success means faithfulness to be and do what God has called me to be and do."

WRAPPING UP

Because our childhood was not perfect, we all came into adulthood with leftover emotions from those early years. Sometimes this is called "emotional baggage" or "unfinished business." These bags can be heavy and loaded with anger, fear, anxiety, insecurity, resentment, shame, hurt, self-contempt, and so on. Pray that God will help you recognize the negative bonds from your past and how they are impacting your present. Ask that he release you from any negative patterns and build into you new patterns of Christlikeness.

GOING DEEPER

- Take some time to sketch a simple genogram of your family over three generations using the questions on page 100 of *The Emotionally Healthy Church*. Include in your diagram as many people as you know. Don't worry about including all of them. Notice any patterns and tendencies (positive and negative) that show up. Share with the group or a friend the positive and negative discoveries you have made.

- Complete the " 'Ten Commandments' of Our Family of Origin" exercise from questions 4 and 8. Review it in your devotional time with God.

FOR NEXT TIME

- Read chapter 7.

Principle 3: *Live in Brokenness and Vulnerability*
Reading: Chapter 7

In Study 3 we saw that the way we do things now is influenced by the way we saw things done in our past. Looking honestly at our families in order to break the power of the past (Principle 2) drives all of us to brokenness.

Living in brokenness and vulnerability means that, in all my relationships, I carry with me the profound awareness and humility that I'm not perfect—that I fall short, and not by a little.

GROWING CONNECTED

Being open and honest is a hard thing to do. It only gets harder when we feel judged, criticized, or backed into a corner.

1. Think of a relationship, small group, or church where you felt safe enough to readily admit your mistakes, accept correction, and talk about your struggles. What ingredients made that place safe for you?

2. Can you think of someone in your life who models brokenness and vulnerability well? Describe them in your own words.

 **STARTERS**

> ### Thorns, Thistles, and Sin . . .
>
> The fall of Adam and Eve has impacted every human being since the beginning of time. We all live in a "cursed" reality geared toward our futility and frustration. Whether in our jobs, relationships, families, or health, it is clear we're a long way from Eden. That is a difficult place to be. Unfortunately, rather than be broken by the thorns and thistles of life and turn to God for our salvation (Gal. 3:21–25), we flee, fight, or freeze.

Flee: We flee when we bury our pain and frustrations by running away. Some people pour themselves into their work to escape a failing home. Other people invest themselves zealously in a church ministry as a way of avoiding difficulty in another area of their life.

Fight: We fight when we blame others and become angry, bitter, or violent because life is not going our way. It doesn't have to be only with people. Think of the times you've been angry with God for not answering your prayers.

Freeze: When we realize that neither fight nor flight will work, we become immobilized. For many people this takes the form of a paralyzing depression. Others find themselves stuck in an unhealthy situation, unable to move.

3. In which of the following situations do you tend to flee, fight, or freeze?

    ____ conflict or tension in your marriage/close friendships

    ____ a stressful deadline at work, home, or ministry

    ____ the unexpected end of a valued friendship

___ financial uncertainty and stress

___ misunderstanding with a coworker or friend

___ an indefinite setback of a personal dream or goal

___ (add your own)

___ (add your own)

4. Share a recent example of how you fled, fought, or froze. Be specific.

BIBLE STUDY

If there was a man who could have chosen to live solely out of his strengths and accomplishments, it was Paul—writer of half of the New Testament, biblical scholar, church-planter extraordinaire, unrivaled missionary, and spiritual father to multitudes. Read 2 Corinthians 12:7–10.

5. Why did God give Paul a thorn in the flesh?

How did it impact his character and life?

6. Describe the kind of person and apostle Paul might have been without this thorn. Imagine a scenario in his life or ministry.

7. What might be a few "thorns" God has entrusted you with?

How have they positively impacted your character and life?

The Corinthians had difficulty grasping Paul's message of "weakness and imperfection." When other "superapostles" arrived at the church in Corinth, they captivated the Corinthians with displays of signs and revelations. Yet, time and time again, instead of appealing to his successes and gifts, Paul chose to "boast in his weaknesses" and live in brokenness and vulnerability.

Spiritual Authority in the Cracks

Paul's theology came out of a conviction that if God was going to use him for his kingdom, he wasn't going to do it through a spiritually polished and puffed-up version of himself, but rather through a broken, limited, and human one. Living in brokenness and vulnerability simply means honestly accepting the fact that I'm not as emotionally put-together or spiritually mature as I would like to think I am. It is embracing "the good, the bad, and the ugly" within myself.

8. Using the list below, or using the full list on pages 120–121 of *The Emotionally Healthy Church,* evaluate your spirituality by circling the answer that tends to describe you.

Proud/Defensive	Broken
1. I am guarded/defensive.	1. I am open/weak.
2. I focus on the "positive," strong, successful parts of myself.	2. I am aware of the weak, needy, limited parts of who I am.
3. I am highly "offendable" and defensive.	3. I am approachable and open.
4. I give my opinion a lot, even when not asked.	4. I am slow to speak and quick to listen.
5. I blame others.	5. I take responsibility for myself and speak mostly in the "I," not the "you" or "they."
6. I am demanding.	6. I assert myself respectfully and kindly.
7. I keep people from really seeing what is going on inside of me.	7. I delight in showing vulnerability and weakness, that Christ's power may be seen in me.

In the areas where you are "Proud/Defensive," can you think of a life experience that reinforced your need to respond in that manner (e.g., a critical father, being misjudged, being gossiped about)? Share one.

In the areas where you are "Broken," how did God build that into your character? Share one example.

 ## APPLICATIONS/EXERCISES

Building a "Résumé of Weakness"

In the world, it is always "best foot forward." Putting together a résumé is often an exercise in creative writing and artistic rendition. We market ourselves through our strengths, accomplishments, and gifts. Yet, this isn't the sort of résumé God is looking for in his disciples.

Below, we're going to get a chance to boast in our handicaps and draft a "Résumé of Weakness." If you need some encouragement, consider a few sample "résumés" of some well-known biblical figures (*EHC*, pp. 129–30):

- John Mark deserted Paul.
- Timothy had ulcers.
- Hosea's wife was a prostitute.
- Jacob was a liar.
- David had an affair, murdered, and abused power.
- Moses was a murderer.
- Jonah ran from God's will.
- Gideon and Thomas both doubted.
- Jeremiah was depressed and suicidal.
- Elijah was burned out.
- Noah got drunk.

Remember, God has been using cracked vessels all through history in order to "show that this all-surpassing power is from God and not from us" (2 Cor. 4:7).

9. Write a first draft of your "Résumé of Weakness" before God.

Name: _____

- **Deficiencies in your training or education:**
  "I never learned how to ..."
  Example: Peter was not professionally trained in the Bible.

- **Missing gifts and/or skills:**
  "I'm not good at ..."
  Example: Moses was a poor public speaker.

- **Obstacles with regard to personality or temperament:**
  "I'm naturally ..."
  Example: Thomas was prone toward skepticism and doubt.

- **Questionable aspects of your past history and testimony:**
  "I used to ..."
  Example: Paul was a former executioner.

■ **Weaknesses in spiritual or emotional maturity:**
"I need to grow in ..."
Example: Abraham needed to grow in faith.

Changing the Culture!

As I began to speak freely of my mistakes, vulnerabilities, and failures, the words "I don't know what to do" became a lot more common in my vocabulary. I talked openly about my insecurities, disappointments, and shattered dreams. In personal conversations, and even from the pulpit, I began to share feelings that I previously had been ashamed to admit—struggles in my own obedience to certain Scriptures, depression, sadness, and confusion. Over time this began to transform the culture of New Life Fellowship. As one person in tears once exclaimed, "I never expected to see anyone, let alone my pastor, that naked!"

---

10. Why is it uncomfortable sometimes to hear the "flaws" and "struggles" of our leaders?

WRAPPING UP

One of the scariest things in the world is to be ourselves. Only by God's grace and by a deep, intimate knowledge of his love and affection can we find the courage to live out a broken and vulnerable life. Pray that God will replace your fears with a surrender to his perfect love.

GOING DEEPER

- Pray through the two styles of leadership: proud/defensive vs. broken/vulnerable. Think of some changes God might be leading you to make so that your life will be characterized more by brokenness and vulnerability.

- Spend time meditating on Rembrandt's painting "The Return of the Prodigal Son" found on page 131 of *The Emotionally Healthy Church*. Also reread pages 130–37. Better yet, purchase and read prayerfully Henri Nouwen's book *The Return of the Prodigal Son* (Doubleday, 1992).

FOR NEXT TIME

- Read chapter 8.

Principle 4: *Receive the Gift of Limits*
Reading: Chapter 8

In Study 4, we learned how God uses the weaknesses of our lives to move in spiritual power and love, and we noted that none of us walks through a fallen world without a few "cracks" to show for it.

As I begin to live in brokenness and vulnerability, I become increasingly aware of my limits. This becomes one of the most difficult lessons to learn in life: that each of us is profoundly limited in who we can be and what we can do, and that these limits are actually a gift from God.

 ## GROWING CONNECTED

1. Some of the most active people in our churches struggle with the discipline of self-care. Imagine four different gas tanks within yourself. Rate where you are in the following tanks. Share one reason why one or more of your tanks is near empty.

Spiritual Tank	Relational Tank	Physical Tank	Emotional Tank
Full	Full	Full	Full
Empty	Empty	Empty	Empty

 **STARTERS**

2. On a scale of 1 – 4 (1 = not true, 2 = sometimes true, 3 = mostly true, 4 = very true), rate yourself on the following:

___ too little time and too much to do

___ constantly feeling pressured or restless

___ feeling inflexible or trapped in your schedule

___ endlessly rushing from deadline to deadline

___ breaking promises of quality time with family or friends

___ never feeling "finished" with work

___ resenting some of your commitments and projects

___ trying to live beyond who you are or what you can do with the limits God has given you

How does this impact your inner joy in God, in your close relationships, and in your service for Christ?

BIBLE STUDY

A Life within Limits

Jesus modeled a life lived within his Father's limits. He fully accepted his humanity and graciously received all the limitations that came with it. He bought food the human way. He rested and slept the human way. Furthermore, although his heart was for the world, Jesus honored the God-given limits of his mission and ministry. As a result, he did not fulfill every need during his short earthly life. He disappointed the crowd's expectations of who he should be. Yet he lived a full life, true and faithful to who he was. He was able to say to his Father: "I have brought you glory on earth by completing the work you gave me to do" (John 17:4). That is God's call for each of us.

---

3. Read Mark 1:32–39. The next morning, needy people were already looking for Jesus. What do you think the disciples thought when Jesus told them they were going to move on to other villages?

Jesus left a town in great need and in the midst of a revival. Often we feel very un-Christlike when we turn away hurting people. But here, Jesus Christ does just that.

4. In what situations is it difficult for you to say no? Why?

5. How did a profound sense of limits allow Jesus to have a sense of completion and satisfaction in his work?

6. During the forty days of testing in the wilderness, the devil repeatedly tried to get Jesus to go beyond the limits the Father had set for him (Matt. 4:1 – 11). In what way(s) is there spiritual warfare raging over your life around the issue of limits?

   What might be some of the consequences if you go beyond what God has asked you to do?

APPLICATIONS/EXERCISES

What Limits Look Like

Limits come in all shapes and sizes. Some are temporary, while others stay with us our entire lives. Some come from the inside, while others come from the outside. A limit can be a situation in life (e.g., an ailing parent), a scar from the past (e.g., bouts of depression because of childhood abuse), a personality trait (e.g., needing lots of alone time to recharge), or a physical reality (e.g., needing eight hours of sleep each night to stay healthy).

---

7. While our culture resists the idea of limits, it is critical that we embrace them. Take a moment and list some of the limits God has given you at this stage of your life. Consider the following categories:

   - personality/temperament
   - number of talents/gifts
   - scars and wounds from your family and past
   - emotional needs and capacity
   - relational status (married or single) and family obligations
   - place where you live
   - finances and resources
   - intellectual capacity
   - spiritual understanding
   - other

Share two or three significant limits God has placed in your life. Instead of seeing these limits as our "enemies," how might they be our "friends" from God?

Faithful to Your True Self

Rabbi Zusya, when he was an old man, said, "In the coming world, they will not ask me: 'Why were you not Moses?' They will ask me, 'Why were you not Zusya?'" The true vocation for every human being is, as Kierkegaard said, "the will to be oneself." (*EHC*, p. 149)

---

8. What do you think it might look like for you to be faithful to your "true self," i.e., the person God uniquely created you to be?

In what way(s) is that more difficult than living out what other people, authorities, or the culture think you should do with your life?

WRAPPING UP

Maturity in life is when we live joyfully within our God-given limits. Take a few minutes and pray for one another that each of you might live a life that fits your God-given nature, a life faithful to your true self, a life that gladly reflects your God-given weaknesses and limitations.

GOING DEEPER

- Meditate on the story "The Bridge" told in the opening of chapter 8 (*EHC*, pp. 139 – 42). What are the relationships in which you may need to draw firmer boundaries in order for you to be true to God's calling for your life? Also, are you the person hanging from the bridge, placing a false expectation and responsibility on another person to "rescue" you from your own life? Explain.

- Pray through the list of limits you made for question 7 and begin to thank God for each one of them. Ask him to show you how to receive them as a gift from him instead of a curse or hindrance.

FOR NEXT TIME

- Read chapter 9.

Principle 5: *Embrace Grieving and Loss*
Reading: Chapter 9

In Study 5, we began to identify and be thankful for each of our God-given limitations. In this study, we are going to see why embracing grieving and loss is such a major theme of Scripture and a central discipleship issue.

God understands that for us, as his image-bearers, learning to grieve is part of maturing in Christ. God himself grieved: "The LORD was grieved that he had made man on the earth, and his heart was filled with pain" (Gen. 6:6). Jesus modeled for us the offering up of "prayers and petitions with loud cries and tears" (Heb. 5:7).

In addition, God has given us an entire book in the Bible called Lamentations. Two-thirds of the Psalms are laments and songs of struggle over loss. In fact, the entire book of Job is a classic struggle with grief and loss.

GROWING CONNECTED

1. Share one personal loss that you have experienced this past year and how it has impacted you.

 **STARTERS**

Loss Is the Norm, Not the Exception

The seasons change, our relationships evolve, children grow up, adults age, churches change—and a part of us misses how things used to be. Other losses come as a result of the choices we make or didn't make. These are the regrets we carry with us. Other losses enter into our lives as a result of the decisions and actions of others—everything from an opportunity denied to a long-felt abuse. What is universal is that we all experience sorrows and are invited to grow through them.

---

2. Our culture resists and avoids grieving. We prefer to get more, smarter, bigger, richer, healthier, happier, and so on. Losses are seen as alien invasions interrupting our "normal lives." As a result, many people live in denial of this reality or seek to medicate themselves to take the pain of life away.

   How did your family of origin deal with losses and setbacks growing up?

   How do you think that may have influenced how you deal with loss and grief today?

3. Share your answers to two or three of the following statements:

"I'm not as _____ as I once was."

"I've never known what it's like to _____."

"I miss _____."

"I did not receive much _____ when
I was growing up."

"A part of me will always be sad that _____."

"Something I wish I had done, but that's impossible now, is
_____."

"When I was younger, I wish I had spent more time
_____."

"I feel a certain amount of regret regarding the way I
_____."

"One thing I miss about my earlier days as a Christian is
_____."

"In the earlier days of our church (or ministry), I loved how we
_____."

Anything but Pain!

I used to believe that grieving was an interruption, an obstacle in my path to serve Christ. In short, I considered it a waste of time, preventing me from "redeeming the time" (Eph. 5:16 KJV) for God. "Just get over it," I would mutter silently to myself ... I was also uncomfortable with the lack of control I might have if I allowed myself to feel the depression, the anger, the sadness, and the doubts about God ...Unable to mourn, I covered over my losses for years and years. (*EHC*, p. 165)

 ## BIBLE STUDY

In spite of enormous time and people pressures during his short earthly life, Jesus took time to grieve his losses and the losses of others. The Jesus of the Gospels is no stranger to his own tears. Make no mistake: the enormous compassion of Jesus was closely related to his being a "man of sorrows" (Isa. 53:3). He allowed the grief of the world to enter into the depths of his heart.

4. In the gospel of John we learn that Jesus enjoyed a close friendship with the family of Lazarus, Mary, and Martha. They sent word to Jesus when Lazarus lay sick, but by the time Jesus arrived, Lazarus was dead. Read John 11:32–37.

   Describe the emotions of Jesus at the news of Lazarus's death.

5. Why do you think Jesus took time to weep over an event he knew he was about to fix?

What does this suggest about his humanity and emotional life?

6. How might your understanding of Jesus be different if he had not wept but instead said: "Come on, everyone, please stop all the moaning. Get a grip. I'll take care of this"?

7. Chapter 9 explores the three phases of the biblical grieving process:

   • Paying Attention
   • Living in the Confusing "In-Between"
   • Allowing the Old to Birth the New

   Which one of these do you find most difficult to do and why?

APPLICATIONS/EXERCISES

Different Lives, Different Losses

In our lives there are at least two types of losses. The first are "Devastating Losses." These are the obvious ones that most people understand to be tragic and sad events—death of children, divorce, abuse, cancer, infertility, a suicide, a betrayal, and so on. Other losses are sometimes called "Insignificant or Natural Losses." These are ones we often stuff down or deny—graduating high school or college, growing older, moving to a new city, changes in your small group or church, and the like. What is universal is that we all experience sorrows and are invited to grieve and grow through them. (cf. *EHC*, pp. 163–164)

---

8. Read the list of losses below. Check the ones you've experienced in your life.

   Devastating Losses:

   ___ death of a child or spouse, family member, or friend

   ___ mental or physical disability

   ___ divorce

   ___ loss of a job

   ___ spousal infidelity

   ___ cancer, disease, illness

   ___ infertility

   ___ suicide in the family

   ___ stillbirth or miscarriage

   ___ shattering of a lifelong dream

   ___ rejection for a promotion or from a school

   ___ other

(Apparently) Insignificant or Natural Losses:

___ church moves to a new building

___ having a child—can't do the things you used to do

___ getting married

___ children moving out of the home

___ entering into old age

___ a close friend or child gets married

___ friends move away

___ small group multiplies

___ a pastor joins or leaves the staff

___ a faithful pet dies

___ retiring from work

___ transferring from one school or job to another

9. Henri Nouwen has rightly said the degree to which we grieve our own losses is the degree to which compassion flows from our lives. Why does that tend to be true?

10. Refer back to the personal loss you mentioned in question 1. How might God be coming to you through that event and/or process?

WRAPPING UP

The path of biblical grieving is a great gift we can give both to ourselves and to others. However, it can often feel as if it is only going to make things worse—as if we shouldn't be going down this road. Yet God assures us that death eventually leads to resurrection. Ask God to give you grace to trust and wait on him as you begin this journey of grieving your losses his way.

 ## GOING DEEPER

- Take a personal "grieving retreat" (*EHC*, p. 176) and make a timeline of the major losses of your life. Ask yourself if you ever took the time to grieve over the events in the timeline. Ask God to begin to show you how to grieve and to lead you through the three-phase process.

- Prayerfully read Psalm 42, 43, 77, or 88. Try writing your own lament psalm to God in which you share your most honest doubts, frustrations, and sorrows with him. Share this with a friend.

FOR NEXT TIME

- Read chapter 10.

Principle 6: *Make Incarnation Your Model for Loving Well*

Reading: Chapter 10

The first five principles of *The Emotionally Healthy Church* are foundational and indispensable to our ability to love well. From taking a deep look inside, to exploring our past history, to finding strength in our brokenness, to receiving our gift of limits, to embracing grieving and loss, God's intention is to transform us in order that we might love well.

Jesus made it clear that love is to be the mark of the church in the world. In this study, we are going to see what it means to love others by following Jesus in his incarnation. Like him you too are called to:

1. Enter another's world

2. Hold on to yourself

3. Hang between two worlds

GROWING CONNECTED

1. Name one person in your life who has loved you well. Describe their qualities.

What caused them to stand out from all the others in your life?

 **STARTERS**

> "Being heard is so close to being loved that for the average person, they are almost indistinguishable."
>
> David Augsburger

Give yourself this short listening test. Check all the statements you can affirm.

____ 1. I make a great effort to enter other people's experience of life.

____ 2. I do not presume to know what another person is trying to communicate.

____ 3. My close friends would say I listen more than I speak.

____ 4. When people are angry with me, I am able to listen to their side without getting upset.

____ 5. People share freely with me because they know I listen well.

____ 6. I listen not only to what people say but also for their nonverbal cues: body language, tone of voice, and the like.

____ 7. I give people my individual attention when they are talking to me.

____ 8. I am able to reflect back and validate another person's feelings with empathy.

____ 9. I am aware of my primary defensive mechanisms when I am under stress, such as placating, blaming, problem-solving prematurely, or becoming distracted.

____10. I am aware of how the family in which I was raised has influenced my present listening style.

____11. I ask for clarification when I am not clear on something another person is saying, rather than attempting to fill in the blanks.

____12. I never assume anything, especially anything negative, unless it is clearly stated by the person speaking.

____13. I ask questions when listening rather than mind reading or making assumptions.

____14. I don't interrupt or listen for openings to get my point across when someone else is speaking.

____15. I am aware, when listening, of my own personal "hot buttons" that cause me to get angry, upset, fearful, or nervous.

If you checked 12 or more, you are an outstanding listener; 8–11, very good; 5–7, good; 4 or fewer, poor. If you want to be really brave, after you score yourself, ask your spouse or closest friend to rate you as a listener. *(EHC, p. 191)*

2. What did you learn about yourself from this experience?

3. What was your experience of being listened to growing up?

How has that influenced you today?

BIBLE STUDY

Jesus in Our Shoes

Jesus modeled incarnating love when he took on flesh, entered our world, and walked in our shoes. His love compelled him to cross two worlds, heaven and earth, and live among us. In order for us to love others as Jesus did, we too need to cross into other people's worlds, enter life in their shoes, while holding on to our own world as well.

Read Philippians 2:5–11.

4. Entering Another's World
    Based on the above passage, what did it cost Jesus to leave heaven and enter our world? (Be specific.)

    What does it cost you and me to leave our reality and comfort to truly "walk in another person's shoes" and enter his or her world?

5. Holding On to Yourself
    Jesus never ceased to be fully God when he became human. In the same way, God does not call us to lose ourselves in an unhealthy way as we enter another's world.

    How can we listen and "be present" with someone, and love them unconditionally, when we do not necessarily agree with them or like what they are saying?

6. Hanging between Two Worlds
   What does the image of Jesus hanging on the cross, between heaven and earth, teach us about loving other people?

7. What is the great promise for us, based on the life of Jesus, if we choose this downward path of incarnational love (see vv. 9 – 11)?

 ## APPLICATIONS/EXERCISES

8. If your group has a person with experience in reflective listening, ask that person to model this for the group in one five-minute exercise as the listener.

   Then, break into groups of two for ten minutes (each of you taking five minutes) and follow the guidelines for listening (see below) based on this question: "What is one thing that has impacted you this week and how did you feel about it?"

As the Speaker
   1. Speak using "I" statements (rather than "you" statements). In other words, talk about *your own* thoughts, feelings, and desires.
   2. Keep your statements brief.
   3. Stop to let the other person paraphrase what you've said.
   4. Include feelings in your statements.
   5. Be honest, clear, direct, and respectful.

As the Listener

1. Give the speaker your full attention (don't be thinking about your rebuttal).
2. Step into the speaker's shoes (feel what they are feeling; then get back out).
3. Avoid judging or interpreting.
4. Reflect back as accurately as you can what you heard them say (paraphrase).
5. When you think they are done, ask, "Is there more?"
6. When they are done, ask them, "Of everything you have shared, what is the most important thing you want me to remember?"

9. (Together as a small group) What was that experience like for you? What did you learn about incarnational loving from this exercise?

WRAPPING UP

Making incarnation a priority can disrupt our lives. Life is no longer simply doing more, "fixing" people, or arranging the world as we see fit. It is about loving well like Jesus. Pray that God will slow you down in order that you might be an incarnational presence to at least one or two people this coming week.

GOING DEEPER

- During this coming week, engage in the discipline of reflective listening with one other person at least one time. You may want to use your own question or the one from the study: "What is one thing that has impacted you this week and how did you feel about it?" Take five to ten minutes as speaker and listener. Afterward, discuss or journal what you learned from the experience.

- Arrange a movie night with your small group to watch the film *Dead Man Walking*. Describe how Sister Helen is able to balance the multiple worlds in which she is engaged. Note how she lives out the three dynamics of making incarnation her model for loving well.

FOR NEXT TIME

- Read chapter 11.

Principle 7: *Slow Down to Lead with Integrity*
Reading: Chapter 11

Most of us are starved for time, overscheduled and preoccupied. Few of us have time to enjoy Jesus, our spouses, our children, or life itself, let alone the gift of leading/serving others. We think, "The space I need for replenishing my soul and relaxing can happen later." There is simply too much to be done.

Slowing down to lead with integrity is a countercultural act of rebellion in our world today. Yet, focusing on the integrity of our relationship with God, ourselves, our spouses, and our leadership is the greatest gift we can give those around us.

GROWING CONNECTED

1. We began this journey into emotionally healthy spirituality by looking beneath the surface and realizing how our "iceberg" shapes the ways we relate to and react to people and situations in our daily lives. What has been your biggest realization, your biggest "aha!" moment, in your walk with Jesus Christ in these past seven studies?

 **STARTERS**

2. Looking back, I can now see the "cracks" that should have alerted me that all was not well. Have you experienced or observed any of these possible warning signs in yourself? Check the ones that apply.

"Spotting the Cracks" List

____ Serving others as a chore, a duty, a burden, instead of a joy

____ Neglecting my inner life with God

____ Seeing people as obstacles rather than gifts

____ Feeling overextended and overworked

____ Constantly serving, doing, and giving, with very little receiving, enjoying, and relaxing

____ Feeling guilty about taking time off for healthy self-care

____ Living spiritually dry and empty

____ Putting out fire after never-ending fire — a crisis-to-crisis lifestyle

____ Lacking the space and time to fulfill commitments and promises

____ Living with a spouse who is lonely or depressed

____ Experiencing an inability to leave work unfinished

____ Denying my problems in front of others

____ Becoming defensive when others criticize or make suggestions to me

____ Pretending not to be resentful, depressed, or angry with someone

____ Feeling isolated from people and disappointed

____ Being unable to let people honestly know what is going on inside me

---

3. If you can identify with any of the "cracks" above, describe one such experience.

BIBLE STUDY

4. Read 1 Timothy 4:7–16. Timothy had been thrust into a position of responsible Christian leadership far beyond his natural capacity. He was young (probably 30–35 years old), prone to illness, shy, and reluctant to lead. Yet he found himself thrust into the responsibility of combating false teachers and bringing order to the church in Ephesus. Paul knows the key to the future of the church centers around Timothy's integrity.

In verse 7, Paul calls Timothy to "train himself" to be godly. In what ways is our life with Jesus Christ similar to an athlete training for an Olympic event?

5. Paul gives Timothy a string of commands in verses 11–16 that culminate in verses 15 and 16: "Be diligent in these matters; give yourself wholly to them, so that everyone may see your progress. Watch your life and doctrine closely. Persevere in them, because if you do, you will save both yourself and your hearers." How do you hear those words for you today?

6. What might be the implications for others if you do, or do not, slow down your life in order to allow Christ to deeply transform you?

 APPLICATIONS/EXERCISES

This diagram provides an illustration of our spiritual life where our activities (e.g., our doing) are out of balance with our contemplative life (e.g., our inner life with Jesus).

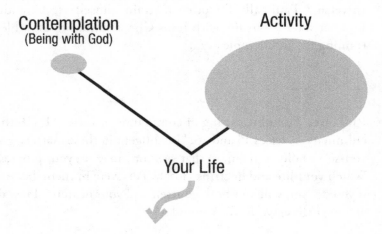

7. Using two circles like the ones above, draw your own diagram to illustrate how your activities (i.e., your doing) balances with your contemplative life (i.e., your being with God).

What challenges keep you from:

- slowing down your life to be with God?

- slowing down your life to care for yourself in a healthy manner as Jesus did (e.g., practicing Sabbath, sleeping adequately, ruthlessly eliminating hurry)?

- slowing down your life to be with your spouse and/or family in a way that honors God?

- slowing down to have integrity in the way you lead others (e.g., being thoughtful with your words, resolving conflicts biblically, remaining aware of God's presence at work)?

8. What might be one or two simple decisions you can make toward taking a first step to slow down your life in one of the above areas?

WRAPPING UP

Take a few minutes and pray together about what God has said to you
during this study.

 ## GOING DEEPER

- Arrange a movie night with your small group to watch *The
  Apostle*. Invite people to share how they related to Sonny's life,
  and what they did or did not appreciate about him.

Conclusion

I trust you can see by now that you have begun a lifelong process that will transform you, your relationship with God, and your relationships with others. Working through this material is challenging, requiring a death to our ingrained destructive behaviors and reactions, and forcing us, in new ways, to explore the truth that will set us free. Nonetheless the fruit is enormously rewarding and rich—beyond anything you can imagine.

WHERE DO YOU GO FROM HERE?

Consider these next steps:
1. See our website, www.emotionallyhealthy.org, to keep abreast of future conferences, retreats, and materials.

2. Sign up for the mailing list for pastors/leaders who continue to be part of this growing movement of leaders committed to integrating emotional health and spirituality. (See above-mentioned website.)

3. Listen to sermons and teachings related to the integration of emotional health and contemplative spirituality so that you can continue to do your own theological and personal work.

4. Read reflectively *Emotionally Healthy Spirituality* (Nelson, 2006) and *Begin the Journey with the Daily Office* (Barrington, IL: Willow Creek Publishing, 2009).

Inventory of Emotional/Spiritual Maturity

Take a few minutes to reflect on this simple inventory to get a sense of where you are as a disciple of Jesus Christ, both as an individual and at church. It will help you get a sense of whether your discipleship has touched the emotional components of your life and, if so, how much.

It is natural to feel uneasy or uncomfortable about some of the questions. Try to be as vulnerable and open as possible. Remember that the inventory will reveal nothing about you that is news to God. Take a moment to pray that God will guide your responses and to remember that you can afford to be honest because he loves you dearly without condition.

Because of space limitations, I have kept Part A to a minimum. I suspect most of you will be far more familiar with the concepts indicated in Part A than in Part B.

PART A:
General Formation and Discipleship

		Not very true	Sometimes true	Mostly true	Very true
1.	I feel confident of my adoption as God's son/daughter and rarely, if ever, question his acceptance of me.	1	2	3	4
2.	I love to worship God by myself as well as with others.	1	2	3	4
3.	I spend regular quality time in the Word of God and in prayer.	1	2	3	4
4.	I sense the unique ways God has gifted me individually and am actively using my spiritual gifts for his service.	1	2	3	4
5.	I am a vital participant in a community with other believers.	1	2	3	4
6.	It is clear that my money, gifts, time, and abilities are completely at God's disposal and not my own.	1	2	3	4
7.	I consistently integrate my faith in the marketplace and the world.	1	2	3	4

TOTAL _____

PART B:
Emotional Components of Discipleship

	Not very true	Sometimes true	Mostly true	Very true

Principle 1: *Look beneath the Surface*

1. It's easy for me to identify what I am feeling inside (Luke 19:41–44; John 11:33–35).   1 2 3 4

2. I am willing to explore previously unknown or unacceptable parts of myself, allowing Christ to transform me more fully (Rom. 7:21–25; Col. 3:5–17).   1 2 3 4

3. I enjoy being alone in quiet reflection with God and myself (Mark 1:35; Luke 6:12).   1 2 3 4

4. I can share freely about my emotions, sexuality, joy, and pain (Ps. 22; Prov. 5:18–19; Luke 10:21).   1 2 3 4

5. I am able to experience and deal with anger in a way that leads to growth in others and myself (Eph. 4:25–32).   1 2 3 4

6. I am honest with myself (and a few significant others) about the feelings, beliefs, doubts, pains, and hurts beneath the surface of my life (Ps. 73; 88; Jer. 20:7–18).   1 2 3 4

TOTAL _____

	Not very true	Sometimes true	Mostly true	Very true
Principle 2: *Break the Power of the Past*				
7. I resolve conflict in a clear, direct, and respectful way, not what I might have learned growing up in my family, such as painful putdowns, avoidance, escalating tensions, or going to a third party rather than to the person directly (Matt. 18:15–18).	1	2	3	4
8. I am intentional at working through the impact of significant "earthquake" events that shaped my present, such as the death of a family member, an unexpected pregnancy, divorce, addiction, or major financial disaster (Gen. 50:20; Ps. 51).	1	2	3	4
9. I am able to thank God for all my past life experiences, seeing how he has used them to uniquely shape me into who I am (Gen. 50:20; Rom. 8:28–30).	1	2	3	4
10. I can see how certain "generational sins" have been passed down to me through my family history, including character flaws, lies, secrets, ways of coping with pain, and unhealthy tendencies in relating to others (Ex. 20:5; cf. Gen. 20:2; 26:7; 27:19; 37:1–33).	1	2	3	4
11. I don't need approval from others to feel good about myself (Prov. 29:25; Gal. 1:10).	1	2	3	4
12. I take responsibility and ownership for my past life rather than blame others (John 5:5–7).	1	2	3	4

TOTAL _____

		Not very true	Sometimes true	Mostly true	Very true

Principle 3: *Live in Brokenness and Vulnerability*

13. I often admit when I'm wrong, readily asking forgiveness from others (Matt. 5:23–24).   1 2 3 4

14. I am able to speak freely about my weaknesses, failures, and mistakes (2 Cor. 12:7–12).   1 2 3 4

15. Others would easily describe me as approachable, gentle, open, and transparent (Gal. 5:22–23; 1 Cor. 13:1–6).   1 2 3 4

16. Those close to me would say that I am not easily offended or hurt (Matt. 5:39–42, 1 Cor. 13:5).   1 2 3 4

17. I am consistently open to hearing and applying constructive criticism and feedback that others might have for me (Prov. 10:17; 17:10; 25:12).   1 2 3 4

18. I am rarely judgmental or critical of others (Matt. 7:1–5).   1 2 3 4

19. Others would say that I am slow to speak, quick to listen, and good at seeing things from their perspective (James 1:19–20).   1 2 3 4

TOTAL _____

	Not very true	Sometimes true	Mostly true	Very true

Principle 4: *Receive the Gift of Limits*

20. I've never been accused of "trying to do it all" or of biting off more than I could chew (Matt. 4:1–11).   1 2 3 4

21. I am regularly able to say no to requests and opportunities rather than risk overextending myself (Mark 6:30–32).   1 2 3 4

22. I recognize the different situations where my unique, God-given personality can be either a help or hindrance in responding appropriately (Ps. 139; Rom. 12:3; 1 Peter 4:10).   1 2 3 4

23. It's easy for me to distinguish the difference between when to help carry someone else's burden (Gal. 6:2) and when to let it go so they can carry their own burden (Gal. 6:5).   1 2 3 4

24. I have a good sense of my emotional, relational, physical, and spiritual capacities, intentionally pulling back to rest and fill my "gas tank" again (Mark 1:21–39).   1 2 3 4

25. Those close to me would say that I am good at balancing family, rest, work, and play in a biblical way (Ex. 20:8).   1 2 3 4

TOTAL _____

Principle 5: *Embrace Grieving and Loss*

Not very true / Sometimes true / Mostly true / Very true

26. I openly admit my losses and disappointments (Ps. 3; 5).   1 2 3 4

27. When I go through a disappointment or a loss, I reflect on how I'm feeling rather than pretend that nothing is wrong (2 Sam. 1:4, 17–27; Ps. 51:1–17).   1 2 3 4

28. I take time to grieve my losses as David (Ps. 69) and Jesus did (Matt. 26:39; John 11:35; 12:27).   1 2 3 4

29. People who are in great pain and sorrow tend to seek me out because it's clear to them that I am in touch with the losses and sorrows in my own life (2 Cor. 1:3–7).   1 2 3 4

30. I am able to cry and experience depression or sadness, explore the reasons behind it, and allow God to work in me through it (Ps. 42; Matt. 26:36–46).   1 2 3 4

TOTAL _____

Principle 6: *Make Incarnation*
Your Model for Loving Well

	Not very true	Sometimes true	Mostly true	Very true
31. I am regularly able to enter into other people's worlds and feelings, connecting deeply with them and taking time to imagine what it feels like to live in their shoes (John 1:1–14; 2 Cor. 8:9; Phil. 2:3–5).	1	2	3	4
32. People close to me would describe me as a responsive listener (Prov. 10:19; 29:11; James 1:19).	1	2	3	4
33. When I confront someone who has hurt or wronged me, I speak more in the first person ("I" and "me") about how I am feeling rather than speak in blaming tones ("you" or "they") about what was done (Prov. 25:11; Eph. 4:29–32).	1	2	3	4
34. I have little interest in judging other people or quickly giving opinions about them (Matt. 7:1–5).	1	2	3	4
35. People would describe me as someone who makes "loving well" my number one aim (John 13:34–35; 1 Cor. 13).	1	2	3	4

Total _____

Principle 7: *Slow Down to Lead with Integrity*

	Not very true	Sometimes true	Mostly true	Very true
36. I spend sufficient time alone with God to sustain my work for God.	1	2	3	4
37. I regularly take a 24-hour period each week for Sabbath-keeping—to stop, to rest, to delight, and to contemplate God.	1	2	3	4
38. Those closest to me would say that my marriage and children take priority over church ministry and others.	1	2	3	4
39. I am not afraid to ask difficult, uncomfortable questions, to myself or to others, when needed.	1	2	3	4
40. I do not divide my leadership into sacred/secular categories. I treat the executive/planning functions of leadership as meaningful as prayer and preparing sermons.	1	2	3	4

TOTAL _____

Inventory Results

For each group of questions on pages 76–83:

- Add your answers to get the total for that group. Write your totals on the top portion of page 85, as the sample on the next page illustrates.

- Next, plot your answers and connect the dots to create a graph on the bottom portion of page 85, again following the sample.

- Finally, see pages 86 and 87 for interpretations of your level of emotional health in each area. What patterns do you discern?

SAMPLE

PART A	Questions	Total
General Formation and Discipleship	1–7	_24_/28
PART B		
Principle 1 *Look beneath the Surface*	1–6	_20_/24
Principle 2 *Break the Power of the Past*	7–12	_11_/24
Principle 3 *Live in Brokenness and Vulnerability*	13–19	_12_/28
Principle 4 *Receive the Gift of Limits*	20–25	_14_/24
Principle 5 *Embrace Grieving and Loss*	26–30	_16_/20
Principle 6 *Make Incarnation Your Model for Loving Well*	31–35	_14_/20
Principle 7 *Slow Down to Lead with Integrity*	36–40	_15_/20

GRAPH

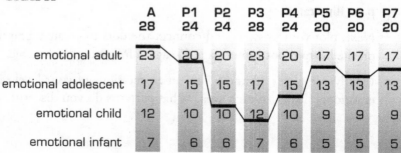

	A 28	P1 24	P2 24	P3 28	P4 24	P5 20	P6 20	P7 20
emotional adult	23	20	20	23	20	17	17	17
emotional adolescent	17	15	15	17	15	13	13	13
emotional child	12	10	10	12	10	9	9	9
emotional infant	7	6	6	7	6	5	5	5

PART A	Questions	Total
General Formation and Discipline	1–7	____/28
PART B		
Principle 1 *Look beneath the Surface*	1–6	____/24
Principle 2 *Break the Power of the Past*	7–12	____/24
Principle 3 *Live in Brokenness and Vulnerability*	13–19	____/28
Principle 4 *Receive the Gift of Limits*	20–25	____/24
Principle 5 *Embrace Grieving and Loss*	26–30	____/20
Principle 6 *Make Incarnation Your Model for Loving Well*	31–35	____/20
Principle 7 *Slow Down to Lead with Integrity*	36–40	____/20

GRAPH

	A 28	P1 24	P2 24	P3 28	P4 24	P5 20	P6 20	P7 20
emotional adult	23	20	20	23	20	17	17	17
emotional adolescent	17	15	15	17	15	13	13	13
emotional child	12	10	10	12	10	9	9	9
emotional infant	7	6	6	7	6	5	5	5

INTERPRETATION GUIDE:
LEVELS OF EMOTIONAL MATURITY

Emotional infants. I look for other people to take care of me emotionally and spiritually. I often have difficulty in describing and experiencing my feelings in healthy ways and rarely enter the emotional world of others. I am consistently driven by a need for instant gratification, often using others as objects to meet my needs. People sometimes perceive me as inconsiderate and insensitive. I am uncomfortable with silence or being alone. When trials, hardships, or difficulties come, I want to quit God and the Christian life. I sometimes experience God at church and when I am with other Christians, but rarely when I am at work or home.

Emotional children. When life is going my way, I am content. However, as soon as disappointment or stress enter the picture, I quickly unravel inside. I often take things personally, interpreting disagreements or criticism as a personal offense. When I don't get my way, I often complain, throw an emotional tantrum, withdraw, manipulate, drag my feet, become sarcastic, or take revenge. I often end up living off the spirituality of other people because I am so overloaded and distracted. My prayer life is primarily talking to God, telling him what to do and how to fix my problems. Prayer is a duty, not a delight.

Emotional adolescents. I don't like it when others question me. I often make quick judgments and interpretations of people's behavior. I withhold forgiveness to those who sin against me, avoiding or cutting them off when they do something to hurt me. I subconsciously keep records on the love I give out. I have trouble really listening to another person's pain, disappointments, or needs without becoming preoccupied with myself. I sometimes find myself too busy to spend adequate time nourishing my spiritual life.

I attend church and serve others but enjoy few delights in Christ. My Christian life is still primarily about doing, not being with him. Prayer continues to be mostly me talking with little silence, solitude, or listening to God.

Emotional adults. I respect and love others without having to change them or becoming judgmental. I value people for who they are, not for what they can give me or how they behave. I take responsibility for my own thoughts, feelings, goals, and actions. I can state my own beliefs and values to those who disagree with me — without becoming adversarial. I am able to accurately self-assess my limits, strengths, and weaknesses. I am deeply convinced that I am absolutely loved by Christ and, as a result, do not look to others to tell me I'm okay. I am able to integrate *doing* for God and *being* with him (Mary and Martha). My Christian life has moved beyond simply serving Christ to loving him and enjoying communion with him.

Get your entire congregation engaged in a new and exciting journey towards emotional health!

Spiritual maturity can only happen once emotional maturity is reached. That's the revolutionary truth Pete Scazzero began to understand as God awakened him to the importance of pursuing a biblical integration of emotional health, a relationship with Jesus, and the practices of contemplative spirituality.

Now you and your congregation can reach beneath the surface to walk the path toward emotional health together with the new *Emotionally Healthy Spirituality Church-wide Initiative kit.*

The complete kit includes:

- One copy of *Emotionally Healthy Spirituality* by Peter Scazzero

- A multi-media pack with message transcripts, teaching notes, promotional materials, campaign training DVDs and more

- One eight-session *Emotionally Healthy Spirituality Small Group DVD*

- One *Emotionally Healthy Spirituality Workbook* for individual or group use

- One *Begin the Journey With The Daily Office* devotional book

emotionally
HEALTHY SPIRITUALITY

For details and quantity discounts, call 800-570-9812 or go to willowcreek.com/ehs

The Emotionally Healthy Church

A Strategy *for* Discipleship *that* Actually Changes Lives

Peter Scazzero
with Warren Bird

Updated *and* Expanded

In this revised and expanded edition of his Gold Medallion Award–winning book, Scazzero shares refreshing new insights and a different and challenging slant on what it takes to lead your congregation to wholeness and maturity in Christ.

Sharing from New Life Fellowship's painful but liberating journey, Scazzero reveals exactly how the truth can and does make you free — not just superficially, but deep down. This expanded edition of The Emotionally Healthy Church not only takes the original six principles further and deeper, but also adds a seventh crucial principle. You'll acquire knowledge and tools that can help you and others:

- look beneath the surface of problems
- break the power of past wounds, failures, sins, and circumstances
- live a life of brokenness and vulnerability
- recognize and honor personal limitations and boundaries
- embrace grief and loss
- make incarnation your model to love others
- slow down to lead with integrity

This new edition shares powerful insights on how contemplative spirituality can help you and your church slow down—an integral key to spiritual and emotional health. Open these pages and find out how your church can turn a new corner on the road to spiritual maturity.

Hardcover, Jacketed: 978-0-310-29335-4

Emotional Healthy Spirituality is a groundbreaking work on the integration of emotional health and contemplative spirituality that current models of discipleship fail to address. Many sincere followers of Christ, followers who are really passionate for God, join a church, participate weekly in a small group, serve with their gifts, and who are considered "mature," remain stuck at a level of spiritual immaturity—especially when faced with interpersonal conflicts and crises. *Emotionally Healthy Spirituality* offers strategies for discipleship that address this void, offering powerful pathways to transformation that will help readers mature into a faith filled with authenticity and a profound love for God.

Share Your Thoughts

With the Author: Your comments will be forwarded to the author when you send them to *zauthor@zondervan.com*.

With Zondervan: Submit your review of this book by writing to *zreview@zondervan.com*.

Free Online Resources at
www.zondervan.com

Zondervan AuthorTracker: Be notified whenever your favorite authors publish new books, go on tour, or post an update about what's happening in their lives at www.zondervan.com/authortracker.

Daily Bible Verses and Devotions: Enrich your life with daily Bible verses or devotions that help you start every morning focused on God. Visit www.zondervan.com/newsletters.

Free Email Publications: Sign up for newsletters on Christian living, academic resources, church ministry, fiction, children's resources, and more. Visit www.zondervan.com/newsletters.

Zondervan Bible Search: Find and compare Bible passages in a variety of translations at www.zondervanbiblesearch.com.

Other Benefits: Register yourself to receive online benefits like coupons and special offers, or to participate in research.